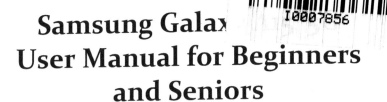

Samsung Gala× User Manual for Beginners and Seniors

The Most Complete & Fascinating User Guide with The Latest Android Tips & Tricks, Coupled with Navigational Screenshots to Help You Harness the Full Potential of Your Device

Tech World

Introduction

Within this comprehensive guide, you will find a wealth of information covering every aspect of your device, from its fundamental features to its more advanced functions. This will enable you to harness the full potential of your gadget.

By making use of convenient methods of communication like phone calls, messaging, and other helpful tools, it is possible to acquire the skill of effectively communicating with family and friends.

Furthermore, the contents of this book offer a novel and insightful perspective that will be highly beneficial to seasoned readers. Without a doubt, clicking the purchase button will be a choice that you will not lament.

Table of Contents

Introduction 4

Turn on your device 15

Use the Setup wizard 17

Bring data from an old device.................................17

Lock or unlock your device 19

    Side key settings 19

    Double press 20

Accounts 20

    Add a Google account..20

    Add a Samsung account......................................21

    Add an Outlook account 21

    Set up voicemail..22

Navigation...23

    Tap 23

    Swipe...24

    Drag and drop 24

    Zoom in and out..25

    Press and hold...26

Navigation Bar 27

    Navigation buttons 27

    Navigation gestures 28

Customize your Home screen....................................30

    App icons..30

Wallpaper...31

Themes...32

Icons..32

Widgets..33

Customize widgets...33

Home screen settings 34

Status bar...37

Notification panel 38

View the notification panel...............................38

Finger sensor gestures......................................39

Quick settings...39

Quick settings options 40

Biometric security..42

Face recognition 42

Face recognition management.........................43

Fingerprint scanner..44

Fingerprint management....................................44

Fingerprint Verification Settings......................45

Biometric settings..46

Edge panels...47

Apps panel 47

Configure Edge panel..49

Edge panel position and style 50

About edge panel..52

Enter text 53

Toolbar 53

Configure Samsung keyboard 56

Smart typing...56

Style and layout 57

Other settings 58

Camera and Gallery 60

Camera...60

Navigate the camera screen 61

Configure shooting modes.............................62

AR Zone 64

Record videos 65

Camera settings 66

Intelligent features 66

Pictures 66

Selfie 67

Videos 67

General 67

Privacy..69

Others 69

Gallery..70

View pictures 70

Edit pictures 72

Play video...73

Edit video 73

Share pictures and videos..............................74

Delete pictures and videos 74

Take a screenshot 75

Screenshot settings..75

Apps 77

Uninstall or disable apps................................77

Search for apps 77

Sort apps 78

Calendar..80

Add calendars 80

Calendar alert styles 81

Create an event..82

Delete an event..82

Contacts 83

Create a contact...83

Edit a contact 84

Favorites 84

Share a contact 85

Show contacts while sharing content.............85

Groups...86

Create a group 86

Add or remove group contacts 87

Send a message to a group 87

Send an email to a group 88

Delete a group 88

Manage contacts 89

Merge contacts 89

Import contacts..90

Export contact..90

Sync contacts 91

Delete contacts 91

Emergency contacts...91

Internet 93

Browser tabs 93

Create a Bookmark 94

Open a Bookmark 94

Save a webpage 94

View history 95

Share pages..96

Secret mode 96

Secret mode settings 96

Turn off secret mode 97

Internet settings 97

Messages 98

Message search 98

Delete messages 99

Emergency messaging 99

Message settings 100

Emergency alerts 100

My Files 102

File groups... 103

My Files settings 103

Phone 105

Calls 106

Make a call 106

Make a call from Recent 106

Make a call from Contacts 106

Answer a call 107

Decline a call 107

Decline with a message 108

End a call 108

Actions while on a call 109

Switch to a headset or speaker............ 109

Multitask 109

Call background 110

Call pop-up settings 110

Manage calls 111

Call log... 111

Save a contact from a recent call........ 112

Delete call records 112

Block a number 112

Speed dial...113

Make a call with speed dial.............................114

Remove a speed dial number 114

Emergency calls 115

Phone Settings 116

Optional calling services 116

Place a multiparty call.....................................116

Video calls 117

Real Time Text (RTT) 117

Settings 119

Access settings...119

Search for settings 119

Connections 120

Wi-Fi..120

Connect to a hidden network 120

Intelligent Wi-Fi Settings.................................122

Advanced Wi-Fi Settings 123

Wi-Fi Direct 124

Disconnect from Wi-Fi Direct..........................125

Bluetooth 125

Rename a paired device 126

Un-pair from a Bluetooth device 126

Advanced options 127

NFC and Payments...128

Tap and pay 128

Airplane mode 129

Mobile networks 130

Mobile Hotspot 131

Configure mobile hotspot settings 132

Auto Hotspot 133

Tethering 134

Notifications 135

App notifications 135

Lock screen notification 135

Notification popup style 136

Do Not Disturb 136

Schedule 137

Allowed during Do Not Disturb 137

Advanced Settings 138

Turn over to mute 140

Display 141

Dark mode 141

Screen brightness 142

Motion smoothness 142

Eye comfort shield 143

Font styles and sizes 143

Screen zoom 144

Full screen apps 144

Camera cutout 145

Screen timeout 145

Accidental touch protection 146

Touch sensitivity 146

Screen saver 146

Double tap to turn on screen 147

Double tap to turn off screen 148

One handed mode 148

Lock screen and security 149

Screen lock types 149

Set a secure screen lock 149

Google Play Protect 151

Install unknown apps 151

Accounts 152

Adding an account 152

Account preferences 153

Remove an account 153

Backup and restore 153

Samsung account 154

Google account 154

External storage transfer 155

Google settings 155

Troubleshooting 155

Software update/System update 155

Reset 156

Reset all settings 156

Reset network settings 156

Reset accessibility settings............................ 157

Factory Data Reset.. 157

Google Device Protection 159

Enable Google Device Protection 159

Disable Google Device Protection 159

Device Layout and Functions

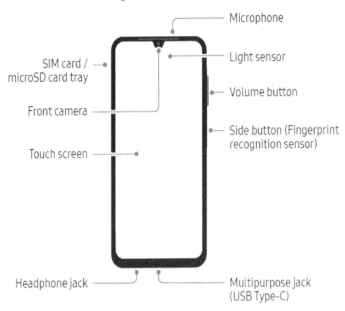

Microphone

SIM card / microSD card tray

Light sensor

Front camera

Volume button

Touch screen

Side button (Fingerprint recognition sensor)

Headphone jack

Multipurpose jack (USB Type-C)

Flash

GPS antenna

Rear camera

NFC antenna (NFC-enabled models)

Main antenna

Speaker

Microphone

Chapter One
Turn on your device

This beautiful device comes with a power button otherwise known as Side key, and it is programmed to perform certain functions like turning it On/Off, lock/unlock the screen, Finger print sensor and many more.

The side key may be used to switch on your device simply by pressing and holding the Side key (Power Key) for a few seconds. Don't use a device if its body is fractured or shattered. Utilize your gadget only when it has been repaired.

- ○ Press and hold the Side button to activate your gadget.
- • When your smartphone is about to shut down, you may confirm by tapping the ⏻ Power off button after simultaneously holding down the volume and Side button.
- • In order to restart your smartphone, press and hold both the volume and side buttons at the same time. When prompted, hit ⏻ Restart.

NOTE: To get the most out of your 5G, you'll need a clean antenna (located on the back of your smartphone) and an optimal 5G connection. You may check with your provider if your network is available; however, the way your device is covered or enclosed may have an impact on how well your 5G performs.

Use the Setup wizard

Setup Wizard will walk you through all of the fundamental setup steps when you first switch on your device.

After choosing your preferred language and connecting to a Wi-Fi network, you may set up your accounts, choose your location service, learn more about the capabilities of your smartphone, and do a lot more by following the instructions.

Bring data from an old device

For the purpose of transferring contacts, music, messages, photographs, notes, videos, calendars, documents, and much more from your old smartphone, you need download the Smart Switch app. Data may be sent from the Smart Switch to a computer, USB cable, or Wi-Fi.

1. Go to Settings, choose Accounts & Backup, then select Bring data from old devices.

2. Then, you pick the items to transfer by following the instructions.

Lock or unlock your device

You may safeguard your cellphone by using its lock screen features. Your smartphone will, by default, lock itself when the screen times out.

Side key/Fingerprint scanner

Press to lock.
Press to turn on the screen, and then swipe the screen to unlock it.

Side key settings

The default shortcuts that are connected to your Side key may always be changed.

Double press

After you double-press your Side button, choose which of these features to use.

1. You should choose ⚙ Advanced features > then Side key from your Settings.
2. To activate this function, click Double Press. Then, touch either of the following options:

- Quick Launch for camera
- Open application by default.

Accounts

Account setup and management are possible.

TIP: Among many other features, your Accounts can handle calendars, contacts, emails, and much more. You can get in contact with the service provider for further information on this.

Add a Google account

To fully utilize the Android capabilities on your smartphone and to access your installed apps and Google Cloud Storage, sign into your Google account. If you establish a lock screen after logging into your Google account. You have turned on Google Device

Protection. This service requires data related to your Google Account in order to restore settings to their original state.

1. You should select 🔄 Accounts & backup > Accounts > Manage accounts from your Settings.

2. After selecting ✛ Add account, select Google.

Add a Samsung account
To fully utilize your Samsung applications and access exclusive content, log into your Samsung accounts.

- o You should select Samsung account from your Settings.

Add an Outlook account
You may manage and see email messages by logging into your Outlook® account.

1. You should select 🔄 Accounts & backup > Manage accounts after selecting it from your Settings.

2. After selecting ✛ Add account, choose Outlook.

Set up voicemail

When you initially open it, you can set up voicemail services. After that, you can access your voicemail using the Phone app. Though your service provider may have various possibilities

1. Press and hold the ⬛ key from within the 🌐 Phone app, or tap 📧 Voicemail.

2. You should first record a greeting, then your name, and last follow the guide for generating a password.

Navigation

For mild touches on your screen using a capacitive pen or your finger pad, the touch screen often functions well. If you contact your touch screen with a metallic object or use excessive force, the surface may get damaged; be aware that your warranty does not cover these types of damages.

Tap

You may softly tap on items to choose or open them.

- Tap on any item to pick it.

- Double-tapping a picture can zoom it in or out.

Swipe

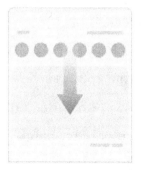

Use your finger to lightly tap and drag the screen.

- To unlock your cellphone, swipe across the screen.

- To access your Home screen or menu settings, swipe the screen of your smartphone.

Drag and drop

Any item may be moved by holding it down and dragging it.

- Drag any shortcut to an application to add it to your home screen.

- You can also drag a widget to reposition it.

Zoom in and out

To zoom in or out, move your thumb and fingers apart or close together rather than directly on top of the screen.

- You should slide your thumb and fingers apart on the screen to zoom in.

- To zoom out, move your thumb and fingers together on the screen.

Press and hold

Touch and hold an object to make it active.

- Press and hold a field to bring up an options pop-up menu.

- Touch and hold a Home screen to personalize it.

Navigation Bar

Using your device's navigation buttons or full screen gesture, you may browse around.

Recent apps ——— ⫶ ⭘ ‹ ——— Back

Home

Navigation buttons

For simple navigation, use the buttons on your bottom screen.

1. Select ⚙ Display > Navigation bar > Buttons from the Settings menu.

2. To choose which side of your screen to display the icons for your recently used and back-up applications, tap on one of the options under Button orders.

Navigation gestures

For a clearer viewing experience, you may conceal the navigation buttons, which are located at the bottom of your screen. Rather than utilizing the navigation on your smartphone, you will swipe.

1. To enable the function, go to Settings, hit ⚙ Display, then Navigation bar, and finally swipe gesture.

2. To personalize your navigation, you can tap on any setting you choose:

• Additional choices: Choose any kind of gesture and sensitivity.

- Gesture tips: This displays lines at the bottom of the screen where the whole gestures can be found.

- Switch apps when hints hidden: If this selection is enabled, you might still be able to move between apps using the gesture when the gesture hints are no longer active.

- Show buttons to hide keyboard: this helps to conceal your keyboard when your device is in portrait mode by displaying an icon at the bottom of your screen.

Customize your Home screen

Typically, you start your navigation from your home. You can always add additional apps, make widgets, and even add more Home screens. You can also change the order of your screens, delete screens, and choose which Home screen to use by default.

App icons

To launch any program from anywhere on your home screen, use its icon.

  o Touch and hold any program icon in the Apps menu, and then tap ⊕ Adds to Home.

To remove an icon:

  o Touch and hold an application icon from anywhere on your Home screen, then hit 🗑 Remove.

NOTE: When you remove an app's icon from your home screen, the app will only disappear from your home screen rather than from your device.

Wallpaper

Your Lock and Home screens may be customized by choosing your preferred images, pre-installed wallpaper, or movies.

1. From any of your home screens, press and hold the screen to choose 🖼 Wallpaper & Style.

2. Tap on any of the options below to view the wallpapers you have available:

- To edit your photographs, tap on them first on your Lock screen and then on your Home screen.

- Choose from my wallpapers: You have a choice of wallpapers to choose from, and you can also download more from your Galaxy Themes.

- Color scheme: Choose a color scheme based on the hues in your wallpaper.

- Adding Dark Mode to Wallpaper: Turn on the Dark mode to add it to your wallpaper.

Themes

Assemble a theme for your app icons, backgrounds, and home and lock screens.

1. You should touch and hold the screen from any of your home screens.

2. To preview and download a theme, hit Tap Themes, and then tap any theme.

3. To access your downloaded themes, select Menu, then My Stuff, and finally Themes.

4. To apply the theme of your choice, choose any theme and then hit Apply.

Icons

To change your default icons, apply a different icon tab.

1. You should press and hold screen from any of your home screens.

2. To preview and download an icon set, select Themes > Icons, and then select the desired icon set.

3. To see the icons you downloaded, press
   Menu > then hit My things > then Icons.

4. To apply the icon set of your choice, press any
   icon, and then select Apply.

Widgets

Add more widgets to the home screens to give quick
access to data or apps.

1. You should touch and hold your screen from
   the Home screen.

2. To access any widget setup, touch on
   Widgets and then tap on it.

3. Swipe over any widget you wish to add to your
   home screen, then hit Add.

Customize widgets

When you're done adding widgets, you may always
change their functionality or where on your Home
screen they appear.

o You should press any choice after holding
   down any widget on your Home screen:

- ⊞ Create stack: Add any widgets to your screen that are the same size so they are stacked in one spot.

- 🗑 Remove: This will get rid of every widget that's there.

- ⚙ Settings: This allows you to personalize your widget's look and functionality.

- ⓘ App information: Check out how you use widgets, the permissions, and more.

Home screen settings

Both your Applications and Home screens are customizable.

1. You should touch and hold the screen from any of your home screens.

2. Select ⚙ Settings and then personalize:

- Layouts for home screens: Set up your smartphone to have separate displays for your applications and home, or to have a single home screen where all of your apps are located.

34

- Grid for home screens: Choose any layout to specify how your icons are arranged on your home screen.

- Grid for Applications screens: Choose any layout to specify how your icons are arranged on your Applications screen.

- Folder grid: To specify the arrangement of your folders, choose any layout.

- Add media pages to your home screen: After this feature is enabled, swipe right to access a media page. To view the accessible media services, tap.

- Show Applications screens buttons in Home screens: This adds a button to your Home screen to facilitate accessing the Applications screen.

- Locks the layouts of your home screen: This helps prevent stuff from being added or deleted.

- Adds new apps to the Home screen: Your Home screen will immediately be updated with newly installed apps.

- Apps on Home & Apps screens may be hidden: Choose which apps to keep hidden from your Home & App displays. To access the hidden apps, navigate to this specific screen. Finder searches might turn up results for hidden apps that are still installed.

- Application icon badges: Enable the badge to be displayed for applications with live alerts. You may also choose the badge's design.

- Swipes down to launch the notifications panel: If this feature is enabled, you may open your notification panel by swiping down from anywhere on your home screen.

- Rotate to landscape mode: When your smartphone transitions from portrait to landscape mode, this feature automatically rotates your home screen.

- About: Look up the version details on the home screens.

- Get in touch with us: A Samsung Member can get in touch with your Samsung support.

Status bar

You can see personal information on the right side of the status bar and device notification alerts on the left.

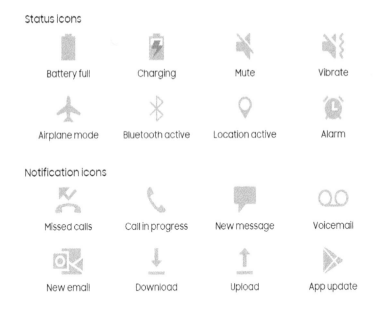

Status icons

Battery full	Charging	Mute	Vibrate
Airplane mode	Bluetooth active	Location active	Alarm

Notification icons

Missed calls	Call in progress	New message	Voicemail
New email	Download	Upload	App update

TIP: To configure your Status bar's notification settings, go to More options > Status bar from the Quick Settings menu.

Notification panel

Just open your Notification panel to get immediate access to settings, notifications, and more.

View the notification panel

Your notification panel is always accessible from any screen.

1. All you have to do is swipe down on your screen to see your notification panel.

- You should tap on any item to open it.

- Drag any notification to the right or left to selectively remove it.

- Press Clear to dismiss all of your alerts.

- You should touch your notification options to personalize your alerts.

2. To shut your, drag up or tap ⟨ from the bottom of the screen.

Finger sensor gestures

You may also use your fingerprint sensor to swipe up and down to open and close the Notification panel.

1. Select ⚙ Advanced features > Motions & gestures > Fingers sensors gesture from your Settings menu.

2. Press 🔋 to initiate the functionality.

Quick settings

Your Notification panel provides rapid access to your device's activities through the use of your Quick settings. The symbols below represent the settings for the most common Quick setting. An icon's color changes whether it's enabled or deactivated. Your device may have other settings accessible.

1. To view your Notification panel, drag down your Status bar.

2. The Quick settings are then visible by swiping down from the top of your screen once again.

- Tapping on it will turn your quick settings icons on or off.

- You may tap and hold the icons to open your quick settings.

| Wi-Fi | Sound | Bluetooth | Auto rotate |
| Airplane mode | Location | Power saving | Dark mode |

Quick settings options

You may access the following options in your Quick settings.

- ⌕Finder search: This feature facilitates device searches.

- ⏻ Power off: Offers choices for both power off and restart.

- ⚙ Open settings: Provides a shortcut to the settings menu on your device.

- ⋮ More options: This modifies the button's layout and lets you rearrange your Quick settings.

- Device control: When a compatible app, such Google Home or Smart Things, is loaded, it can control any other device.

- Media output: this opens your Media panel and manages linked audio and video playing.

- Brightness slider: This tool lets you change the brightness of your screen by dragging it.

Biometric security

You may use your fingerprint to unlock and safeguard your smartphone, as well as to log into your account or any other sensitive application.

Face recognition

Turn on your facial recognition software to unlock your screen. To utilize your smartphone's face unlock feature, you must first set up a PIN, pattern, or password.

- Your facial recognition is still less secure than passwords, PINs, and patterns. It may be anybody or anything that looks like you that unlocks your smartphone.

- Face recognition may be hampered by some things, such as wearing hats, spectacles, beards, or extensive makeup.

- Before registering your face, make sure the lens of your camera is still clean and that you are in a well-lit area.

1. After selecting ⚪ Security & privacy > from your Settings, choose Biometrics > before Face recognition.

2. To register your face, follow the instructions.

Face recognition management

Tailor your facial recognition to your preferences.

○ Select ⚪ Security & privacy from your settings, then Biometrics and finally Face recognition.

• Remove faces data: This eliminates any faces that are already there

• Face unlocks: You may turn on and off your security and facial recognition.

• Remain on Lock screens till you swipe: Use facial recognition to unlock the smartphone, then remain on Lock screens until you swipe.

• Brighten screen: This momentarily brightens your screen to make it easier to see your face in dimly lit areas.

- About Face Recognition: Learn more about use your facial recognition to secure devices.

Fingerprint scanner

You may use your fingerprint recognition in certain applications in place of inputting passwords.

You may also use fingerprints to verify who you are while logging into your Samsung account. Before you can use your fingerprint to unlock your smartphone, you must first create a PIN, password, or pattern.

1. Select ⬤ Security & Privacy > Biometrics > Fingerprints from the Settings menu.

2. To register your fingerprint, follow the instructions.

Fingerprint management

It is possible to rename, remove, and even add fingerprints.

   o To access the following options, go to Settings > ⬤ Security & privacy > Biometrics > Fingerprints.

44

- At the top of this list is the list of fingerprints that have been registered. A fingerprint can be removed or renamed by tapping on it.

- Register more fingerprints: To register more fingerprints, simply follow the instructions on your device.

- Verifies newly added fingerprints: This scans the fingerprint to see whether it has already been registered.

Fingerprint Verification Settings

Use fingerprint recognition to authenticate yourself while utilizing compatible apps and actions.

- o Tap on ⬤ Security & privacy from your settings, then choose Biometrics > then Fingerprints.

- Fingerprint unlocking: This method uses your fingerprint to verify who you are anytime you unlock a device.

- Always-on fingerprint scanning: This feature enables fingerprint scanning even while your screen is off.

- Use to log in to websites: Logs in to websites using fingerprints.

- Uses for Samsung account verifications: You may use your fingerprints to authenticate yourself in place of entering your password for your Samsung account.

Biometric settings

Use biometrics to configure the security features that you want.

- To access these choices, go to Settings > Security & privacy > and choose Biometrics.

- Displays unlock transition effects: When you use your fingerprint to unlock your smartphone, transition effects will appear.

- About biometric unlocking: Learn more about how to secure your phone using biometrics.

Edge panels

Edge panels are made up of many customizable panel types that are easily accessible from the edge of your screen. Edge panels may be used to read news, sports, and other information in addition to accessing tasks, contacts, and apps.

- o To enable this function, select Display > Edge panels from your Settings menu then tap

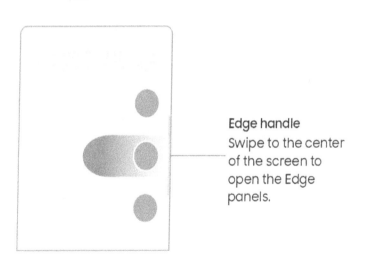

Edge handle
Swipe to the center of the screen to open the Edge panels.

Apps panel

Applications are always welcome additions to your Apps panels.

1. You should drag the Edge handle to move it to the center of your screen from any part of it. Next, swipe to bring up your Apps panel.

2. To open an application or pair of applications, tap on their shortcuts. For a complete list of all applications, you can also touch on ⦙⦙⦙All apps

- To launch more windows in the pop-up view, drag the icon of your program from the Apps panel onto the screen that is now active.

To configure the Apps panel:

1. From anywhere on your screen, drag the Edge handle to the center of your screen, slide to show your Apps panel.

2. To add more apps to your Apps panel, use the ✏Edit button.

- To add an application to your Apps panel, find it on the left side of your screen and press it to add it to the open space in the right column.

- You should drag any program from your left side screen at the top of any application from the columns by the right in order to create folder shortcuts.

- You may rearrange the applications on your panel by dragging and dropping them in the desired order.

- Tap the ▬ Remove button to get rid of any program.

3. In order to save your edits, tap ‹ Back.

Configure Edge panel.

It's always possible to personalize your Edge panels.

1. Press ⚙ Display > then Edge panels > then Panels from your Settings.

2. The options are as follows:

- ✓ Checkbox: This lets you turn each panel on or off.

- Edit (if available): This sets up each panel separately.

- ○ Search: Look for panels that are installed or that are ready for installation.

- ⋮Additional choice:

  - Reorders: This modifies the arrangement of your panels by dragging them to the left or right

  - Uninstall: This gets rid of the Edge panel that was installed on your phone.

  - Hides on Locks screens: When you enable secure screens lock, this feature allows you to choose which panels to hide on your lock screen.

- Galaxy Store: You may use this to look for and download more Edge panels from your Galaxy Store.

3. To save your edits, you should press the ‹ Back button.

Edge panel position and style

You may adjust where the Edge handle is located.

  o To access the following options, select ⊙ Display > Edge panels > Handle from your Settings menu:

- Edge handle: To change the location of your Edge handle, drag it along the edge of your screen.

- Position: Choose the Left or Right option to determine the orientation of your Edge screen.

- Lock handles positions: When this feature is on, it helps keep your handles from shifting when they are touched and held.

- Style: Choose your Edge handle's color scheme.

- Transparency: This drags your slider to adjust the transparency of your Edge handle.

- Size: Drag your slider to adjust the size of your Edge handle.

- Width: Drag your slider to change the width of the Edge handle.

- Vibrates when handle is touched: The Edge handle will emit a vibration upon contact.

About edge panel

You may view licensing information and the installed software version from your Edge panel features.

○ Select Edge panels > then About Edge panels from your Settings by tapping on Display.

Enter text

You may either use your voice or your keyboard to enter your text.

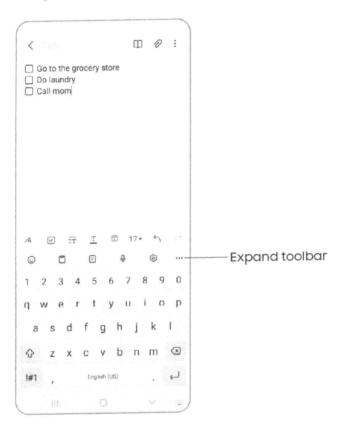

Expand toolbar

Toolbar

The toolbar offers quick access to your keyboard's functionality. Depending on the service provider, options vary.

- On your Samsung keyboard, press ••• to see more options by expanding your toolbar:

- ☺ Expression: Experiment with various emoji types, GIFs, make original mixed emojis, and much more.

- ⌸ Clipboard: To go to the clipboard you use.

- ⊡ One-handed keyboards: Converts keyboard layouts to one-handed operation.

- 🎤 Voice input: Use the voice inputs on your Samsung device.

- ⚙ Settings: This button opens the keyboard's settings.

- ⌨ Split keyboards: This modifies your keyboard to a divided, split version.

- ⌨ Floating keyboards: This modifies your keyboard so that it seems to float and can be positioned anywhere on the screen of your device.

- Search: This retrieves particular words or phrases from your exchanges.

- Translate: Type words or sentences to have them translated into different languages using the keyboard.

- Grammarly: This allows you to type while receiving suggestions from Grammarly.

- Emojis: Emoji inserting made easier.

- GIFs: Compile the animated GIFs.

- Bitmoji: This tool assists you in making your own customized emojis that you may use as stickers.

- Mobitok: This app lets you add automatically suggested stickers or makes your own custom stickers.

- AR Emoji: This tool lets you make your own customized emoji and then utilizes it as a sticker that you may select from.

- ⬜ Keyboard sizes: You may change the height and width of your keyboard.

- ◇ Text editing: This lets you select the text you want to copy, paste, or trim using an editing panel.

Configure Samsung keyboard

Adjust the settings on your Samsung keyboard.

○ To access these options, swipe left on your Samsung keyboard and select ⚙ Settings:

- Languages & Types: Choose the languages that are available on your keyboard after setting up the type of keyboard you use.

- You may slide your space bar to the right or left to change between languages.

Smart typing

- Predictive texts: See suggested words and phrases as you type.

- Suggested Emoji: Include emojis when using predictive text.

- Offers a sticker suggestion as you type: Peruse the suggested stickers while you type.

- Auto replace: This function automatically inserts recommended text in lieu of your input.

- Makes correction recommendations for text: Underline misspelled words in red and propose changes.

- Text shortcuts: Create shortcuts for frequently used words and phrases.

- More Typing Option: Provides additional customization choices for typing.

Style and layout

- Keyboard toolbars: This allows you to show or hide the keyboard toolbar.

- High contrast keyboards: These can let you fine-tune the color and size of your Samsung keyboard to improve the contrast between the background and your keys.

- Themes: Allows you to customize the keyboard's theme to anything you choose.

- Mode: This feature allows you to choose between portrait and landscape mode.

- Sizes & Transparency: Give you flexibility in adjusting the keyboard's size and transparency.

- Layout: This makes the numbers on your keyboard stand out with different characters.

- Type sizes: To change the size of your type, drag on your slider.

- Custom symbols: Lets you modify the keyboard shortcuts for symbols.

Other settings

- Voice inputs: Configures the services and settings for your voice input.

- Touch, swipe, and feedback: This lets you personalize your motions and responses.

- Screenshots may be saved to the keyboard clipboard by using the "Save to Clipboard" feature.

- Allows the use of third-party content: Approves the usage of third-party keyboards.

- Resets to defaults: This feature removes all customized data and lets you go back to your initial keyboard settings.

- About Samsung keyboards: View the version and all the legal details pertaining to the keyboard you own from Samsung.

- Contact us: Assists you in contacting a Samsung Member to reach the Samsung support team.

Chapter Two

Camera and Gallery

You can take excellent photos and films with your Camera app. Images and movies that are saved in your Gallery can be viewed and edited.

 Camera

Enjoy all of the high-level video modes, pro lenses, and pro settings.

    ○ Tap the Camera from your Apps.

TIP: To effortlessly open your Camera app, double tap the Side key.

Settings

Zoom

Shooting modes

Switch cameras

Gallery

Capture

Navigate the camera screen

Take amazing pictures using your device's front and back cameras.

1. You may set up your shot from your 📷 camera by utilizing the following features:

- Press the screen's center button to bring the camera into focus.

- A brightness scale appears on your screen as soon as you tap. To change your brightness, use the slider.

• Swipe up or down on your screen to quickly swap between your front and back cameras.

• To zoom in at a certain level, hit the 1x and then select any choice from the screen's bottom. (This feature is limited to utilizing your back camera.)

• You may slide your screen right or left to switch to a different shooting mode

• You should tap on ⚙ Settings to change the camera settings.

2. Press the ◯ Capture button.

Configure shooting modes

By doing this, you may choose from a variety of shooting settings and let the camera choose the one that will provide the finest images.

○ To switch between shooting modes, slide your screen left or right from your 📷 Camera.

- Portrait: This enables you to add backdrop elements to pictures that are portrait-oriented.

- Photo: adjusts the settings on your camera to get the greatest shots.

- Video: enables your camera to choose the ideal settings for your recordings.

- More: Assists in choosing from a variety of shooting modes. Press ⊕ to add and move modes to and from the shooting modes trays located on your camera's bottom screen.

- Pro: Enables you to manually alter the exposure value, color tone, white balance, and ISO sensitivity even when shooting images.

- Macro: Assists in taking a close-up photo of a subject that is three to five centimeters away.

- Panorama: Allows you to take pictures in either a horizontal or vertical orientation to produce linear images.

- Night: Enables you to take photos without using your flash in dimly lit environments.

- Cuisine: Captures images that accentuate the vibrant hues of any cuisine.

- Slow motion: This makes it easier to capture films at a high frame rate for slow motion viewing.

- Hyperlapse: This feature allows you to record at a variable frame rate and produce time-lapse videos. Your device's motions and the scene being recorded will determine how your frame rate is adjusted.

AR Zone

Access all of the augmented reality (AR) features in one location.

o To activate the AR Zone, slide to More from your Camera and tap it. Among the features offered are:

• AR Emojis Studio: Makes use of AR capabilities to create and modify My Emoji avatars.

• AR Emojis Stickers: These are added to My Emojis avatars as AR stickers.

- Deco Pic: This feature lets you use your camera to instantly embellish images and movies.

Record videos

Your device's camera may be used to capture smooth, endearing videos.

1. To move to a video filming mode, you should slide left or right from your 🔘 Cameras.

2. To begin recording any video, simply tap the ◦ Record button.

- Tap on 🔘 Capture to take pictures while you're filming.

- Tap ‖ Pause to momentarily stop recording. Next, press ◦ Resume to start your recording again

3. When you're done recording, tap ■ Stop to end the recording.

Camera settings

Use the icons on the settings menu and on the camera's main screen to adjust the settings.

○ To access the following options, tap on Settings from your ◉ Camera:

Intelligent features

- Scene optimizers: These automatically modify the color scheme of your pictures to better suit the topic.

- Scannable QR codes: When your camera is in operation, this feature automatically finds QR codes.

Pictures

- Swipes on Shutter buttons to: This lets you choose whether to take continuous images or to turn your shutter motion into a GIF once you swipe to the nearest edge.

- HEIF images: Assists in saving your photos to your storage as high-quality images. Some sharing websites might not accept this format.

66

Selfie

- Save the selfies as preview: This feature allows you to save selfies without them flipping when they appear on your preview.

Videos

- High efficiency videos: Assists in saving your videos in HEVC format. Some devices or sharing websites might not be able to play the format.
- Video stabilization: Turn on anti-shake to keep your focus constant while your camera moves.

General

- Auto HDR: This lets you get more information about bright or dark regions in your picture.
- Grid lines: To help with composition while taking pictures or videos, display the grid lines in your viewfinder.
- Position tags: Add GPS position markers to your photos and videos.
- Method of shooting:

- Pressing the Volumes key: Use your volume keys to take pictures, record movies, enlarge images, or change the volume on your computer.

- Adding a second moveable shutter button that can travel across your screen is a great way to add floating shutter buttons.

- Showing palms: Your picture will be taken in a few seconds if you extend your hand and face the camera with the palms facing up.

• Setting up to keep: Choose whether to launch Camera in the same selfie orientation, with the same filters, and in the same photographic mode as the last time.

• Storage location: This feature allows you to designate a location for keeping your images and movies.

- You must add any microSD card—which was not included—in order to view the location of your storage.

- Shutter sounds: When you take a photo, this plays a sound.

Privacy

- Review Samsung's privacy regulations. View the required and optional permissions for the Camera application.

Others

- Resets settings: Clear the settings on your camera.

- Contact us: To get in contact with Samsung support, use Samsung Members.

- About Camera: Get details about software and applications.

 Gallery

To access all of the visual media you have stored on your smartphone, navigate to your Gallery. It is possible to view, edit, and manage images and movies.

- You should select ✻ Gallery from your Applications.

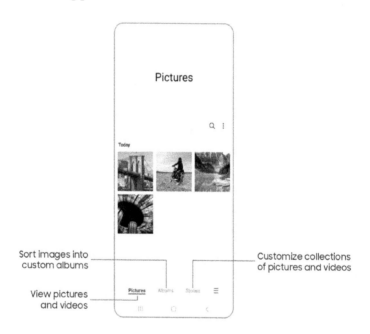

View pictures

You may use your Gallery application to see the stored photographs on your smartphone.

1. Select the Images by tapping on them from your ✱ Gallery.

2. You may see photographs by tapping on them. Next, swipe to the right or left to view any further images or videos.

- Tap ♡ Adds to Favorites to add any photo to your list of favorites.

- Choose ⋮ further choices to obtain the following features:

- Details: Enables you to examine and edit the metadata for your photograph.

- Copy to clipboard: This feature enables you to copy and paste a picture into an alternative program.

- Set as wallpaper: Choose your image to serve as your background.

- Print: Upload your image to any connected printer.

Edit pictures

To make your photos seem better, use the editing tools in your Gallery.

1. Select Pictures from your ✱ Gallery.

2. After tapping any image to view them, you should tap ✎ Edit to see the options below:

- 🗐 Transform: Modify the overall appearance of the picture by cropping, rotating, flipping, or using other effects.

- ◎ Filters: Enables you to accumulate color effects.

- ☼ Tone: Adjust the brightness, contrast, exposure, and other parameters.

- ☺ Decorations: Feel free to add text, stickers, or any other hand-drawn artwork.

3. Revert: To restore your original photo, undo the changes that were performed.

4. After finished, you should hit the Save.

Play video

Check out the videos stored on your device. Videos may be favorite and watched in detail.

1. Click on the Pictures from your ✳ Gallery.

2. Tap a video to watch it. Swipe to the right or left to view more images or videos.

3. To add a video to your list of favorites, tap ♡ Adds to Favorites. The video is now available in the Favorites area of your album.

- Tap more choices to get the following features:

- information: Assists in seeing and editing video information.

- Set as wallpapers: Assist you in setting a video as the background of your lock screen.

4. To play your video, use the ▶ Play button.

Edit video

To modify stored movies on your device

1. Tap any video from your ✳ Gallery.

2. To see any video, tap on it.

3. To remove a section of your video, tap ✎ Edit.

4. When asked, tap "Save," and then confirm.

Share pictures and videos

You may share images and movies using the Gallery app

1. You may touch on a picture from your ✹ Gallery.

2. To share a photo or videos, choose ⋮ More choices > Edit and select the one you want to share.

3. After tapping on "⤴ Share," choose an application or connection to share the content you've chosen. Observe the instructions.

Delete pictures and videos

The images and movies that are saved on your device can be removed

1. Select Edit from your ✳ Gallery by tapping on
   ⋮ More choices

2. To choose pictures and videos, tap on them.

3. Press 🗑 Delete, and when asked, confirm the
   action

Take a screenshot

Snap a picture of the display. Your device's Gallery
app will immediately create a new album called
Screenshots.

o Press and hold the Side and Volume down
  keys from any part of your screen.

Screenshot settings

You may always change the settings for your
screenshots.

o Select ⚙ Advanced features > then
  Screenshots from the Settings menu.

• Toolbars appear after capturing: When you
  are taking a screenshot, extra options are
  displayed.

- Screenshots are immediately erased after being shared using your screenshot toolbar. This happens automatically.

- Hide status and navigation bars: Assists in concealing your status or navigation bars.

- Format: Select whether you would want to save any of your screenshots as PNG or JPG files.

Chapter Three
Apps

All of the downloaded and preloaded apps are displayed in your apps list. You may get your application from the Google Play and Galaxy stores.

- o You may access your Apps list by swiping upward from any Home screen.

Uninstall or disable apps

Any application on your smartphone can be removed at your discretion. It could only be possible to deactivate some preloaded programs, or the accessible default apps on your smartphone. Apps that are disabled will first be hidden from your Apps list before being turned off.

- o You may press the Uninstall/Disable button after holding down a program in your Apps

Search for apps

You may use your Search function to discover any program or configuration that you are unsure of where to look

1. You should select 🔍 Search from your Apps and then input a term or words. A results screen displays when you type in programs or settings that match.

2. To open the program, tap the result.

TIP: Tapping on ⁝ More choices > then Settings will always allow you to change the search parameters.

Sort apps

You have the option to rearrange the list in a different order or to have your app shortcuts shown alphabetically.

- o To access the following sorting options, select ⁝ More options > then Sort from your Apps menu.

- • Custom order: This option allowed you to manually arrange apps.

- • Sort your applications using the alphabet as a guide.

TIP: You may eliminate the empty spaces between your icons when apps are manually ordered (custom

order) by pressing ⋮ More settings > then Cleans up
pages.

Calendar

To combine all of your calendars in one location, the Calendar program may establish connections with all of your several internet accounts.

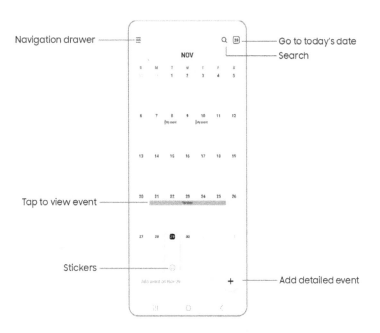

Add calendars

Your Calendar program allows you to add several accounts.

1. Press and hold the≡ Navigation drawer from within your⬛ Calendar.

2. Press Manage calendars, then click ╋ Add account and select any kind of account.

3. After entering your account details, adhere to the instructions.

TIP: In addition to other capabilities, your accounts could support contacts, email, and other data.

Calendar alert styles

Users of the Calendar application can personalize the alert style.

1. You should touch on ☰ Navigation drawer from your ⊡ Calendar, then ⚙ Calendar settings, and finally Alert style. The choices that are accessible are as follows:

- Light: Receive a notification and hear a short sound.

- Medium: A complete screen alert is displayed along with a short sound.

- Strong: A full-screen notice and ring sound will sound when you dismiss it and will not stop until you do so.

2. Based on the alert style you have chosen in the past. The following audio selections are available:

- Short sound: For your Light or Medium alert categories, choose your alert sound.

- Extended sound: Choose the alarm sound that best suits your Strong alerts style.

Create an event

Make use of your calendar to create events.

1. To add an event, select ⊕ Add detailed events from your 🗓 Calendar.

2. After entering your information for that event, hit Save.

Delete an event

Events on your calendar are removable.

1. You should tap any event in your 🗓 Calendar then tap it again to update it.

2. When asked, tap 🗑 Delete and confirm.

Chapter Four

Contacts

Keep and organize your contact list. It could synchronize with personal accounts you've connected to your device. Accounts may also provide calendars, email, and other functions.

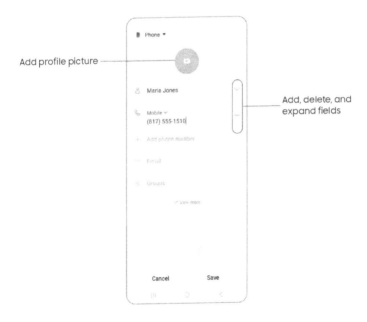

Create a contact

1. Select "+Create contact" from your  Contacts.

83

2. After entering your contact's information, click Save.

Edit a contact

You may add additional fields to the list of details for any contact you are updating, or you can touch on a field to modify or remove data.

1. Tap on a contact from your list of 👤 Contacts.

2. Click the ✏️ Edit button.

3. Click on any of your fields to edit, remove, or add data.

4. Click the Save button.

Favorites

Contacts that you have marked as favorites will always appear at the top of the contact list, giving you easy access to them from other apps.

1. Tap on a contact from your 👤 Contacts.

2. To make that contact one of your favorites, tap on the ☆ Favorites.

- Tap on ⭐ Favorites to take any contact out of your Favorites.

84

Share a contact

Any contact may be shared with others using a range of sharing services and methods.

1. You should tap on a contact from your contacts.

2. Click the Share button.

3. Select the text or vCard (VCF) file to tap on.

4. After deciding on a sharing strategy, adhere to the instructions.

TIP: While browsing the contact, choose More > then QR code to easily share contact data with friends and family. Your QR code automatically updates when you make changes to your contact information fields.

Show contacts while sharing content

You may rapidly share your stuff with contacts from within any application. Once activated, your frequently used contacts appear on your Share window.

o To enable this option, go to Settings >
Advanced features > Show contacts while
sharing contents, and then tap .

Groups

The groups may be used to arrange your connections.

Create a group

You are able to make your own contact groups.

1. You should choose Show navigations menu
   > then Groups from your Contacts.

2. After selecting "Create group," you may write
   information about the group by tapping on
   the fields:

   • Group name: You may give your new group
     whatever name you like.

   • Customize your group sound for the ringtone.

   • Add member: Click Done once you've selected
     which contacts to add to the newly formed
     group.

3. Click the Save button.

Add or remove group contacts

You may add or remove contacts from a group as often as you'd like.

- ○ Select Groups from the ☰ Shows navigations menu by tapping on it, and then tap on a group in your 👤 Contacts.

- • Press and hold any contact to select it, then select 🗑 Remove to eliminate it.

- • You can add any contact by tapping ✎ Edit >, choosing Add member, and then tapping on the contact you want to add. After completion, select Done > and then Save.

Send a message to a group

Group members can receive text messages from you.

1. You should select ☰ Show navigations menu > Groups from your 👤 Contacts, then touch on a group.

2. Select " ⋮ More options" > "Send message."

Send an email to a group

To the people in your group, you send emails.

1. Select the ☰ Shows navigations menu > Groups > 👤 Contacts > and then select a group by tapping on it.

2. Select "⋮ More options" and then "Send email."

3. Select contacts by tapping on them, or select all by tapping the All option at the top of the screen, and then select Done.

- Only individuals with a personal email address on file are shown as group members.

4. Select any email account you own, then adhere to the instructions.

Delete a group

To remove any group that was formed, carry out the following procedures.

1. Touch the ☰ Shows navigations menu > option from your 👤 Contacts, choose Groups, and then touch on a group.

2. After selecting⋮ More choices, tap Delete group.

- Select Delete groups only to remove a group exclusively.

- Tap on Delete groups & shift members to trash to remove your group and all of its contacts.

Manage contacts

Contacts may be exported or imported, and several contacts can be linked into a single contact record.

Merge contacts

Consolidate many sources of contact information into a single contact. When entries are combined into a single interaction

1. Tap the ☰ Shows navigations menu > option from your 👤 Contacts, then choose Manage contacts.

2. Select "Merge contacts" by tapping. The contacts with the same phone number, email

address, and name will then be shown together.

3. After choosing your contacts with a press, select Merge.

Import contacts

Contacts can be imported onto a device as vCards files (VCF).

1. Select≡ Shows navigations menu > then Manage contacts from your 👤 Contacts list.

2. After selecting Import contacts, follow the instructions.

Export contact

Contacts may be exported as vCard files (VCF) for your devices.

1. Select Manage contacts after tapping on≡ Show navigation menu from your 👤 Contacts.

2. After selecting Export contacts, follow the instructions.

Sync contacts

You can keep all of your accounts' contacts up to date.

1. Select Manage contacts after tapping the ☰ Shows navigations menu from your 🧑 Contacts.

2. Press the Sync contacts button.

Delete contacts

One contact or several contacts can be deleted at once.

1. You should touch and hold any contact in your 🧑 Contacts, then choose it.

• To pick, you may also tap on any other contacts that you like to remove

2. Press 🗑 Delete, and when asked, confirm the action.

Emergency contacts

You may still call your emergency contacts even if your smartphone is locked.

- Select Safety & emergency > then Emergency contacts from your Settings.

- Add member: You may designate contacts as emergency contacts on your smartphone.

- Shows on the Locks screens: Provides quick access to your emergency contacts in case of an emergency by displaying them on your Lock screens

Chapter Five

 **Internet**

For your mobile device, the Samsung Internet is a trustworthy, quick, and easy-to-use web browser. To take use of improved web browsing features, use the Contents Blocker, Biometric Webs Login, and Secret Mode.

Browser tabs

Tabs are a useful tool for viewing many web pages at once.

- ○ Select ⬜ Tabs > then New tab from your 🔘 Internet browser.

- • You should touch on ⬜ Tabs > to ⊗ Close tab in order to close any tab.

Create a Bookmark

You should bookmark your favorite websites so you can access them quickly.

- ○ To maintain your open webpage, you should click the ☆ Add to favorites button on your 🔘 Internet.

Open a Bookmark

Any website may be readily accessed from your Bookmarks page.

1. Click on ☆ Bookmarks from your 🔘 Internet browser.

2. Click the bookmark entry.

Save a webpage

You have several options in your Samsung Internet application to save any webpage.

o To access the following options, select ☰ Tools > then Add page from your ◎ Internet browser.

- Bookmarks: Include a webpage in your collection of favorite websites

- Easy access: View a list of websites that you bookmark or often visit.

- Home screen: Create a shortcut to your webpage from the Home screen.

- Saved pages: These are webpages that are stored on your device and may be accessed offline.

View history

You may see a list of the websites you have recently visited:

o To access your ◎ Internet, select ☰ Tools > then History.

TIP: Tap ⋮ More options > Clear history to completely erase your browsing history.

Share pages

Web sites may always be shared with people on your contact list.

- From your ⬡ Internet, touch ☰ Tools >, choose Share, and then adhere to the on-screen instructions.

Secret mode

Viewed pages in secret mode don't leave any cookies or other traces on your mobile device, nor do they show up in your search or browser history. Secret tabs have a richer hue than conventional tab windows.

Such downloaded files remain on the device after you shut your hidden tab.

1. Select ☐1 Tabs > Turn on your hidden mode from your ⬡ Internet.

2. To begin browsing in hidden mode, tap Start.

Secret mode settings

To enter secret mode, use a password or biometric lock.

1. Click on ⬚ Tabs from your ⬤ Internet browser.

2. For these choices, tap ⋮ More options > and then your Secret modes settings:

- Use Password: Create a password in order to access secret mode and use biometrics.

- Reset Secret mode: This removes all data kept in secret mode and returns default settings.

Turn off secret mode

You may always go back to your normal surfing after disabling secret mode.

o You should select ⬚ Tabs > Turn off the hidden mode from your ⬤ Internet.

Internet settings

Your Internet application's settings are modifiable.

o Select ≡ Tools > then Settings from your ⬤ Internet browser.

Messages

Send hellos, share photos, and send emoticons with people you know using the Messages app to keep in contact. Service providers could present a range of choices.

Message search

You may use your search function to locate a message with ease.

1. You should select ⌕ Search from inside your 💬Messages.

2. Enter search terms in the designated field and press the ⌕ Search key on your keyboard.

Delete messages

By ending talks, you may get rid of your conversion history.

1. You should select More options > Delete from your 💬 Messages.

2. For each chat you want to end, tap on it.

3. Press "🗑 Delete all," and when prompted, confirm the action.

Emergency messaging

You may send messages, including audio and photo attachments, to all of your emergency contacts.

○ Press your key five times to initiate these measures. From your Settings, select 🛡 Safety & emergency >Emergency SOS.

- Countdown: Choose the number of seconds you wish to wait before initiating emergency protocols.

- Place an emergency call: Choose the number to contact in an emergency.

- Information sharing with emergency contacts: Enable the feature that lets your emergency contacts know where you are.

TIP: You may also press down on your Side & Volume button and then touch on 🔵 Emergency call to activate your Emergency SOS.

Message settings

You have the ability to customize the parameters for both text and multimedia communications.

○ Select ⋮ More options > Settings from your 🔵 Messages.

Emergency alerts

Your emergency notifications inform you to impending dangers and other situations. You won't be charged for your emergency alert texts.

o To personalize your notifications for your emergency alerts, go to Settings > Safety & emergency > Wireless Emergencies Alerts.

TIP: The Notifications section is where you can also view your emergency notifications. To enable Wireless Emergency Alert, hit Notifications from your options, then click Advanced options.

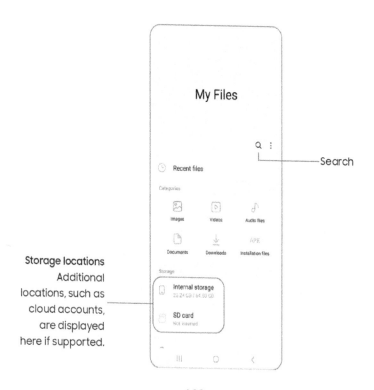 My Files

Items stored on your device may be managed and viewed; these items might include papers, sound snippets, music, movies, and much more. When enabled, you may also access and manage the data kept on your SD card and in cloud accounts on your smartphone.

My Files

——— Search

Storage locations
Additional
locations, such as
cloud accounts,
are displayed
here if supported.

File groups

The following groups comprise the files that are saved on your device:

- Recent files: Provides access to the files you've lately utilized.

- Categories: Allows you to examine files according to their type.

- Storage: Provides access to data from your device's memory card, cloud accounts, and optional storage.

- The services you are signing up for may have an impact on your Cloud accounts.

- Analyze storage: Determines what is using up space on your device.

My Files settings

To customize your file management choices and much more, use the My Files options. Depending on your service provider, these choices could vary.

- Select Settings by tapping on ⋮ More choices from your ⬭ My Files folder.

- Cloud accounts: Aids in managing and connecting to cloud services
- File management: You always have the option to change how your files are displayed, removed, or even accessed via your mobile data.
- Analyze storage: This feature lets you mark files of any size when you examine your storage.
- Privacy: Permits you to examine My Files' permissions.

Chapter Six

Phone

You can do more with your Phone application than just place calls; you can also take use of its sophisticated calling capabilities. You can contact your service provider for further information. Depending on your service provider, your phone application's screen appearance and accessible settings will change.

Access voicemail

(311) 555-2368

Make a video call

Make a call

Calls

You may make and receive calls using your phone application from the Contacts, Recent, and Home screens of your smartphone, among other places.

Make a call

From any panel on your home screen, you may use your phone to make and receive calls.

- From your ⓒ Phone, input any number onto the keyboard and press 📞 Call.
- If your keypad is not visible, tap on it.

Make a call from Recent

Your call log contains a record of every call you make and receive, as well as missed calls.

1. To view a list of your most recent calls, choose Recent from your ⓒ Phone.

2. After tapping on a contact, you tap 📞 Call.

Make a call from Contacts

Any contact listed in your Contacts app is available for calls.

o You may call any contact by swiping your finger towards the right from within your Contacts.

Answer a call

Your phone will ring when someone calls, and then the caller's name or number will appear on the screen. You will get a pop-up screen for your incoming call if you were using another program when you received the call.

o To answer your call, drag the Answer button to the right on the screen of incoming calls.

TIP: To answer your call, hit Answer on the pop-up screen that appears when one is inbound.

Decline a call

You could be using another program, and you may choose to reject any incoming calls. Your incoming call will be shown on a pop-up screen.

- To reject an incoming call and send it to your voicemail, drag the ⌢ Decline button to the left of the screen on the call screen.

TIP: To reject a call and send it to your voicemail, simply hit the ⬤ Decline button on the incoming pop-up screen.

Decline with a message

You can choose to send a text message in response to any incoming call, declining it.

- On the screen of your incoming calls, drag the Send message button to the upper right and select a message.

TIP: Tap Send message and select a message from the pop-up box that appears when you get a call.

End a call

- When you're ready to stop a call, tap ⬤ stop call.

Actions while on a call

Changing the speaker or headset on your call, adjusting the call volume, and even performing other tasks while on the call

o   To adjust the volume, press the buttons on your device.

Switch to a headset or speaker

You have two options for listening to your call: utilizing your Bluetooth® headset (which is not included) or using your speaker.

o   Press ◁)) Speaker to hear the caller through your speaker, or press ⁂ Bluetooth to hear the caller through any Bluetooth headset.

Multitask

The status bar will display the status of your active call when you switch from the call screen to another app.

To return to the call screen:

o   To view your notification panel, drag your status bar down. Then, touch on the call.

To end a call while multitasking:

o To view your Notification panel, drag your Status bar lower. Then, hit 🌑 End call.

Call background

Select an image or video to play when a call comes in or goes out.

o To access these choices from your ⓒ Phone, touch ⦙ More options, then choose Settings, and finally Call background:

• Layout: Define how caller details are shown when the user has a profile photo.

• Background: Choose an image to display while you're on the phone.

Call pop-up settings

You may see pop-up windows for calls when you're using other apps.

o When utilizing apps, you should choose Call display by tapping on ⦙ More options > Settings > from your ⓒ phone. These are the options that are accessible below:

- Full screens: Assists in displaying incoming calls across the whole screen of your Phone app.
- Tiny pop-up: When a call comes in, a pop-up appears at the top of your screen.
- Little pop-up: When a call is incoming, display a little pop-up.
- Keep calls on pop-up: Enable this function to keep calls on your pop-up window even after they have been answered.

Manage calls

Your calls are documented in your call log. You have the option to set up your speed dials, use voicemail, and block numbers.

Call log

The phone numbers you may have phoned, missed, and received are all recorded in your call log.

o You should press Recent from your Phone. A list of recent calls is displayed. If your caller is on your list of Contacts, their name will show.

Save a contact from a recent call

Use the information from a recent call on the Contacts list to add or edit a contact.

1. Select Recent with a tap from your ⓒ Phone.

2. After touching the call with the information you want to save in the Contacts list, hit Add to contacts

3. To add a new contact or update an existing one, select the corresponding option.

Delete call records

You may always remove entries from your call logs:

1. On your ⓒ Phone, press the Recent icon.

2. To erase a call from your call log, touch and hold the desired call.

3. Press the 🗑 Delete button.

Block a number

Any calls from that number won't go to voicemail in the future, and you won't get any messages if you add them to your banned list.

1. From your ⓒ Phone, select Recent and press.

2. To add a caller to your block list, touch on them and then select ⓘ Details.

3. To block a contact, either touch ⊘ Block or More > Block contact, and then confirm when prompted.

TIP: You may also change your Block list's settings. You should choose Block numbers after tapping More choices, Settings, and then ⁝ More options from your ⓒ Phone.

Speed dial

A shortcut number can be provided to a contact so they can quickly call that number.

1. Press the Keypad icon on your ⓒ Phone, then pick ⁝ More from the menu, and finally choose Speed dial number. Your saved speeds dial number is shown on your screen of speed dial numbers.

2. Press any random number.

- Press ▼ Menu to select a different Speeds dial number from the following number in the series.

- The first voicemail is reserved for voicemail.

3. Enter any name or number to link a contact to a number, or touch to 👤 Add a contact from your contacts.

- Your selected contact is displayed in your speed dial numbers bar.

Make a call with speed dial

You may make phone calls with Speed Dial.

- You should touch and hold your Speed dial numbers from your 🄲 Phone.

- If your speed dialed number contains more than one digit, enter the first few numbers and hold the last digit.

Remove a speed dial number

You can take away a Speed dialed number that has been assigned.

1. From the ⓒPhone menu, choose More options > and then select Speed dial numbers.

2. By pressing ⎯ Delete, choose the contact you want to take off of your speed dial.

Emergency calls

You can dial the local emergency number regardless of the state of service on your phone. When your phone is off, the only calls you can make are emergency ones.

1. To initiate a call, dial your emergency number (911) from your ⓒPhone and press the Call button.

2. Finish the call. You may use most of the in-call features when on this type of call.

TIP: You may use your phone to contact emergency services during an emergency by calling your emergency number, even if it is locked. When the caller's screen is locked, the only features they can access are your emergency call capabilities. The phone is still completely guarded.

Phone Settings

These options allow you to modify the settings of your phone application.

- o You need to select More choices > then Settings from your ⓒ Phone.

Optional calling services

Your service package and cellular carrier may support these calling services.

Place a multiparty call

Make another call while you're on the phone. Service providers could present a range of choices.

1. To place a second call, hit ╋ Add call any called from your current call.

2. Enter your new phone number and then choose 📞 Call. As soon as someone answers your call:

- Press the ⬑ Swap or Hold Down button to quickly switch between two calls.

- To listen to both of your callers at once, tap ≫ Merge. (many conferences)

Video calls

Use these during video calls:

o   Enter any number into the 🅲 Phone and then
select 🎥 Meet or 🎥 Video Call, if not ⭕
Video Call altogether.

NOTE: Not all devices can make video calls. The caller has the option to accept the video call or answer the call using traditional voice.

Real Time Text (RTT)

You and another person may type back and forth in real time while on a call.

You can use RTT when you make a call to someone whose phone is either compatible with RTT or connected to a teletypewriter (TTY). Every incoming signal has your RTT symbol.

1.   You may tap on ⋮ More choices > the Settings from your 🅲 Phone.

2.   To access the following settings, tap on Real-time texts:

•   RTT call buttons: Choose any visibility setting that you'd like for your button.

117

- Use an external TTY keyboard: Ensure that your RTT keyboard is hidden while using an external TTY keyboard.

- TTY mode: Choose your favorite TTY style from your keyboard.

Chapter Seven
Settings
Access settings

There are several methods to access the settings on your smartphone.

- You should swipe down from any part of your Home screen and then hit on ⚙ Settings.

- Navigating to Applications, you should choose ◉ Settings.

Search for settings

If you are not sure where a setting is exactly, you can search for it.

1. Select 🔍 Search from your Settings and type in your search terms.

2. To access the setting, tap on any entry.

Connections

Control the connections that your device makes to various networks and other devices

Wi-Fi

You may use a Wi-Fi network to connect your device and surf the Internet without using any of your mobile data.

1. To activate your Wi-Fi and search for accessible networks, navigate to Connections > Wi-Fi from your Settings and press .

2. When prompted, tap on a network and enter a password.

3. Press the Connect button.

Connect to a hidden network

If a scan is unable to locate the specified Wi-Fi network, you can still join by entering its information by hand. Ask the Wi-Fi administrator of your network for the name and password before you begin.

1. To enable Wi-Fi, navigate to 🛜 Connections > Wi-Fi from your Settings and then hit the ⏵ button.

2. At the very bottom of your list, tap ╪ Add network

3. Enter your Wi-Fi network's information here:

- Network name: Specify your network's exact name here.

- Security: Select the security option from your selection, and when prompted, enter your password.

- Password: Enter the password for your network.

- Hidden networks: These are networks that you may insert into.

- See more: Enter IP and proxy settings, among other complex factors.

4. Click the Save button.

TIP: Scan a QR code using your device's camera, then press the ▦ Scan QR code to connect to Wi-Fi.

Intelligent Wi-Fi Settings

You can manage your stored networks, find the network address on your smartphone, and establish connections to various Wi-Fi and hotspot types. Service providers could present a range of choices.

1. Select 🛜 Connections > Wi-Fi from your Settings, then tap 🔵 to turn on your Wi-Fi.

2. Select ⋮ More options > and then utilize these settings for Intelligent Wi-Fi:

   • Flip to mobile data: When your Wi-Fi connection is unstable, your smartphone will always utilize mobile data if this function is enabled. When the strength of your signal is high, it returns to Wi-Fi.

   • Wi-Fi auto-turn on or off: It activates your Wi-Fi in locations you visit regularly.

   • Auto-Hotspot connections: The device will automatically establish a connection with a Wi-Fi hotspot upon detection.

   • Intelligent Wi-Fi: Verify the available version of this feature.

Advanced Wi-Fi Settings

You can manage your stored networks, find the network address on your smartphone, and establish connections to various Wi-Fi networks and hotspots. Service providers could present a range of choices.

1. To enable your Wi-Fi, navigate to Connections > Wi-Fi from your Settings and then hit the button.

2. Press More options, choose Advanced settings, and then make use of these settings:

- Synchronize with Samsung Cloud or account: Link your Samsung account and Wi-Fi profiles together.

- Wi-Fi/network notifications: Receive alerts anytime open networks are found within range.

- Manage networks: Access the stored Wi-Fi networks and select which ones to remember or automatically rejoin to.

- History of Wi-Fi on and off: Find out which apps have most recently turned on or off your Wi-Fi.

- Hotspot 2.0: Connect to Wi-Fi networks automatically while utilizing those that support Hotspot 2.0.

- Network certificate installation: Assists in the installation of network authentication certificates.

Wi-Fi Direct

Wireless data sharing between devices is made possible via Wi-Fi Direct.

1. To enable your Wi-Fi, navigate to Connections > Wi-Fi from your Settings and then hit the ▶ button.

2. After tapping on ⋮ More choices, choose Wi-Fi Direct.

3. Press the device, then adhere to the connection instructions.

Disconnect from Wi-Fi Direct

To unplug from any WIFI Direct device, take the following actions:

- Go to Settings, hit ⬡ Connections, then Wi-Fi, then press ⋮ More choices, and finally choose Wi-Fi Direct. To disconnect from that device, tap ⬗ .

Bluetooth

You may link your device with other Bluetooth-enabled devices, such Bluetooth headphones or in-car entertainment systems. Once a pairing has been made, the devices will remember each other and transfer data without needing to enter the passkey again.

1. To enable Bluetooth, navigate to ⬡ Connections > Bluetooth from your Settings, then hit the ⬗ button.

2. To connect, tap on a device and then follow the on-screen instructions.

TIP: To take advantage of this function, tap Bluetooth while sharing any file.

Rename a paired device

To make any associated device easier to identify, you have the option to rename it.

1. To enable Bluetooth, navigate to Connections > Bluetooth from your Settings, then tap to activate Bluetooth.

2. Select Settings by tapping the circle around the name of your device, and then select Rename.

3. After entering a new name, choose Rename.

Un-pair from a Bluetooth device

When you un-pair your Bluetooth device from another device, the two devices will no longer recognize one another, and you will need to pair them again in order to connect to that device.

1. To enable your Bluetooth, navigate to Connections > Bluetooth from your Settings and press it.

2. After selecting ⚙️Settings, which is located next to your device, you should select Un-pair

3. For confirmation, press on Un-pair.

Advanced options

There are additional Bluetooth functions available in your Advanced menu. Service providers could present a range of choices.

1. Press on 📶 Connections > then Bluetooth from your Settings.

2. You may either press the Advanced settings or ⋮ More choices >, then choose Advanced setting and make use of these options:

- Synchronize with Samsung Cloud or account: You have the option to sync files that are sent to your Samsung account over Bluetooth.

- Ringtone synchronization: Select the ringtone that is set up on your device when a call comes in on a Bluetooth-connected device. ⬚⬚History of Bluetooth Controls: View the apps that have recently utilized Bluetooth.

- Requests for blocking pairings: Add more devices to the list of blocked pairs.

- Manage your Bluetooth features application and view which apps have recently looked for nearby Bluetooth devices using Bluetooth scanning history.

NFC and Payments

NFC (Near Fields Communication) allows you to talk to another device without connecting to a network. A similar mechanism is used by Android Beam and other payment applications. Both your handset and the device you are broadcasting to need to support NFC and be four centimeters apart.

- To activate this option, go to Settings, hit Connections, choose NFC & contactless payments, and then tap to confirm.

Tap and pay

Using an NFC payment application, you may make payments by pushing your device against a credit card reader that is compatible.

1. To enable NFC, navigate to 📶 Connections > NFC & contactless payments from your Settings, then touch 🌙.

2. To access your default payment application, tap on Contactless payments.

- You should touch on any accessible application to pick it in order to use the use an alternative payment application.

- You should touch on Pay using the currently open application in order to utilize an open payment application.

- To set up a different payment service as your default, hit Others, then select the preferred option.

Airplane mode

When your smartphone is in airplane mode, all network connections are deactivated, including Bluetooth, Wi-Fi, mobile data, calling, and messaging. When Airplane mode is active, you may use your Quick Settings pane or Settings to activate both Bluetooth and Wi-Fi.

o Select 🛜 Connections from your Settings, then Airplane mode. Tap 🌙 to activate the function.

NOTE: The use of cell phones aboard ships and airplanes may be subject to local, state, and federal rules and restrictions. When in airplane mode, there will be no network access available. Disabling ultra-wideband (UWB), which is prohibited on board ships and aircraft, may be done via airplane mode. When determining how and when to use the equipment, pay close attention to crew instructions and get confirmation from the appropriate authorities.

Mobile networks

To configure your device to use mobile data and connect via mobile networks, make use of your mobile networks. Service providers could present a range of choices.

o Select 🛜 Connections > then Mobile networks from your Settings.

• Mobile data: Activate the use of your mobile data.

- International data roaming: this modifies the international roaming settings for text, phone, and data roaming.

- VoLTE calls: Use LTE to provide improved communication.

- Names of Access Points: Choose or add APNs with the network configurations your device needs to connect to your provider.

- Network operators: Select the desired networks out of those that are accessible.

- Diagnostics for mobile networking: Compile usage statistics and diagnostics to aid in troubleshooting.

TIP: Use these services for assistance in controlling connection settings that may affect your monthly bill.

Mobile Hotspot

Your mobile hotspot makes use of your data plan to create Wi-Fi networks that many devices may connect to.

1. Select 🛜 Connections > Mobile hotspot & tethering > Mobile hotspot from the Settings menu.

2. To make your mobile hotspot active, tap 🌙.

3. Turn on the Wi-Fi on the device you want to connect to, then choose the Wi-Fi hotspot on your device. Enter the mobile hotspot's password to establish a connection.

- Under the title "Connected devices," connected devices will be listed.

TIP: Scan the ▦ QR code with your device to connect to the mobile hotspot instead of typing in the password.

Configure mobile hotspot settings

You may always change your mobile hotspot's security and connectivity settings.

1. To access mobile hotspot, go to Settings > 🛜 Connections > Mobile hotspot & tethering > Mobile hotspot.

2. Press Set to access these configurations:

- Network name: View and change the name of your Wi-Fi hotspot.

- Password: A password is required in order to access or change your security level.

- Band: Select one of the available bandwidth options.

- Security: Decide how secure the mobile hotspot is.

- Advanced: Configure additional hotspot parameters.

Auto Hotspot

Other devices linked to your Samsung account will instantly be able to access your hotspot connection.

1. Select Connections > Mobile hotspot & tethering > Mobile hotspot from your Settings.

2. To activate the function, first tap Auto hotspot, and then tap .

Tethering

To share the device's internet connection with another device, use tethering. Service providers could present a range of choices.

1. You should select Mobile hotspot & tethering by tapping on Connections from your Settings.

2. Select any menu item:

- You may use Bluetooth tethering to share your device's internet connection with other people.

- You can use a USB cable to connect your computer to any device, and then you can enable USB tethering.

- Use an Ethernet adapter to connect your computer to your device, and then choose Ethernet tethering.

Notifications

By changing which applications send notifications and how you get them, you may prioritize and optimize application alerts.

App notifications

You may choose which applications get notifications.

○ To enable notifications for individual applications, navigate to Notifications > App notifications from your Settings and press to activate them.

Lock screen notification

On your lock screen, you may choose which notification you want to receive.

○ To enable the function, tap Notifications > Locks screens notifications after selecting it from your Settings. Press one of the customizable options:

• Content hiding: Stop alerts from showing up in your Notification panel.

- Show notifications: Choose which alerts you want to see appear on your lock screen.

Notification popup style

You may customize the extra features and the design of your alerts.

- Open Settings, press ⬤ Notifications, choose Notifications pop-up styles, and choose any pop-up style you like:
- Brief: This lets you personalize your alerts.
- Apps to show as brief: Choose which applications to show as a quick alert.
- Edge lighting styles: Assists in choosing the aesthetic of the edges lighting for your alerts.
- Colors by keyword: Choose custom colors for alerts that contain terms that you find significant.
- Detailed: Activate your Samsung's default notifications setting.

Do Not Disturb

When in the "do not disturb" mode, you have the option to disable audio and notifications. You may also make exceptions for certain people, applications, and alerts. It is also feasible to schedule routine tasks like meetings and sleeping.

- ○ Select 💬 Notifications > Do-not disturbs from your Settings, then configure these:
- Do not disturb: Enable "Do not disturbs" to turn off notifications and noises.
- How much time is it? You may choose your default duration when you manually enter the Do Not Disturb mode.

Schedule

- Sleeping: Establish a customized sleep schedule for the "Do not disturb" setting.
- Include a schedule: Establish a new practice to determine the days and times when you should regularly turn off your phone's notification light.

Allowed during Do Not Disturb

- Messages & Calls: Tap to allow Do Not Disturb exceptions.

- Notifications from applications: Include the apps you wish to get alerts from when in "Do-Not Disturb" mode. You will continue to get call, message, and chat notifications even if you refuse access to the relevant applications.

- Noises and alarms: You may activate vibrations and noises for events, reminders, and alarms when your "Do not disturb" setting is in effect.

- Conceal alerts: Go to the customization settings to conceal your alerts.

Advanced Settings

Notification settings are configurable through your applications and services.

- o Select Notifications > Advanced settings from the Settings menu.

- Displays notification icons: You may change how many alerts appear in your Status bar.

- Displays battery percentages: Your smartphone's Status bar will indicate how much battery life it presently has.

138

- Notification history: Display the most recent and snoozed alerts.

- Conversations: See alerts pertaining to the ongoing discussions. Touch and hold a conversation notification to mute it, make it alert, or make it priority.

- Floating notifications: Choose whether to enable the notifications that float between Bubbles and the Smart pop-up displays.

- Action recommendations and message responses: Get pertinent action recommendations in response to alerts and messages.

- Show snooze button: This feature enables you to quickly snooze alerts by displaying a button.

- Reminders for notifications: Turn on and customize automated reminders for alerts from certain apps and services. Go through and delete your alerts to turn off the reminders.

- Application icon badges: Find out whether applications have badges that appear in their icons as a means of indicating which ones have current alerts. You may tap to choose whether the number of unread notifications appears on your badges.

- Wireless Emergencies Alerts: Customize your choices for receiving emergency alert alerts.

Turn over to mute

You may flip your iPhone facedown and silence incoming calls and alerts.

o Select Advanced features > Motions & gestures > Turn over to mute, then press on to activate from your Settings.

Display

In addition to many other display options, you can always adjust the text size, brightness of your screen, and timeout delay.

Dark mode

You may switch to a significantly darker theme using the Dark mode to assist your eyes relax at night and with bright screens, dimming white, and alerts.

o To access these settings, navigate to Settings and choose Display.

• Light: Assists in applying light color themes to the device (by default).

• Dark: Assists in setting the device's theme to dark hues.

• Settings for Dark Modes: Allows you to choose where and when to apply your Dark mode.

- Activates on schedule: Configures your Dark mode to activate between sunset and morning on a custom timetable.

Screen brightness

Adjust the screen's brightness to suit your lighting conditions or personal preferences.

1. Choose Display from your Settings by tapping on it.

2. Change the options under Brightness:

- To adjust the brightness level to your liking, drag the Brightness slider.

- To assist you automatically adapt the brightness of your screen based on your lighting circumstances, tap the "Adaptive brightness" button on your screen.

TIP: The Quick settings window gives you the option to change the brightness of your screen.

Motion smoothness

Increasing your screen's refresh rate will make your animations seem more realistic and make scrolling easier.

1. Choose Motion smoothness by tapping on Display > from your Settings.

2. After selecting any option, touch Apply.

Eye comfort shield

This function may reduce glaucoma and enhance your slumber. It is possible to arrange the automatic on and off of this function.

- o Open your Settings, press Display >, choose Eye Comfort Shield, and then choose one of the following options:
- To use this feature, tap on .
- Select Always on, custom, or Sunset to Sunrises after tapping on Set schedule.
- To adjust the opacity of your filter, drag on the skidder of your color temperature.

Font styles and sizes

To customize your device, you may choose the font styles and sizes.

- o To access these choices, touch on Display > from your Settings, then choose Font size & style:
- Press Font style to select an alternative font.

- Select a font by tapping it, or add fonts from the Galaxy Store by tapping + Download fonts.

- To apply bold weight to all fonts, tap Bold font.

- To change the text's size, use the Font size slider.

Screen zoom

You can simply see your material by adjusting the zoom level at any time.

1. Go to Settings, choose ⚙ Display, and then select Screen zoom.

2. To change the zoom level on your screen, use the zoom sliders.

Full screen apps

You may choose which apps to run in aspect-ratio full-screen mode.

- To enable this feature with your customized preferences, touch on apps after selecting Full screens applications from your Settings screen.

Camera cutout

You may use a black bar to hide the area with your camera cutout.

o To enable this function and adjust settings, go to Settings, touch ⚙ Display, then Camera's cutout, and finally press Applications.

Screen timeout

You may set your screen to turn off after a predetermined amount of time.

o To set it up, go to Settings, touch ⚙ Display, then Screens timeout, and finally press on any time limit.

NOTE: Prolonged motionless picture display—that is, images that are not moving—may result in ghostly afterimages or permanently degraded image quality (with the exception of Always On Displays). When your display screen is not in use, turn it off.

Accidental touch protection

This will stop your device's screen from reacting to touch inputs while it's in a dark area, such as your pockets or bags.

  o To enable this function, go to Settings, tap on Display, and then choose Accidental touch safeguards.

Touch sensitivity

Let's utilize screen protectors in conjunction with an increased touch sensitivity setting for your screen.

  o To activate this function, go to Settings, touch Display, and then choose Touch sensitivity.

Screen saver

Screen savers allow you to see images and colors while your device is charging or while it is off.

1. You should select Display > then Screen saver from your Settings.

2. Choose any of the following:

• None: There won't be a screen saver visible.

146

- Colors: To see a screen that changes color, tap your selection.

- Photo table: Displays pictures on the table.

- Picture frame: Display images within picture frame

- Photos: Displays pictures from the Google Photos library.

3. To see a demo of the screen saver of your choice, tap Preview.

TIP: To access further settings, tap the ⚙ Settings button that appears next to it.

Double tap to turn on screen

Double-tapping your screen will turn it on instead than using your Side key.

- o To enable this function, go to Settings, press on ⚙ Advanced features, choose Motions & gestures, and then double tap the screen to toggle it on.

Double tap to turn off screen

Instead of using your Side key to turn off your screen, you may double-tap it.

o   To activate this function, go to Settings, press on ⊙ Advanced features, then select Motions & gestures. Finally, double tap the screen to turn it off.

One handed mode

You may change the arrangement of your screen to make it suitable for one-handed use of your mobile device.

1. Choose One-handed mode by tapping on ⊙ Advanced features > from your Settings.

2. After tapping ⫸ to enable the function, select one of the following options:

•   Motion: You should swipe down from the bottom border of the screen in the middle.

•   Button: To decrease the size of your display, swiftly tap ⬜ Home twice.

Lock screen and security

You may secure and safeguard your smartphone by turning on a screen lock.

Screen lock types

The following are the screen lock types that offer medium, high, or no security: Password, Pattern, PIN, Swipe, and None.

NOTE: You may also use your biometric locks to safeguard private information on your smartphone and stop illegal access.

Set a secure screen lock

It is advised that you use a secure screen lock (password, PIN, or pattern) to protect your device. This is required in order to activate and configure biometric locks.

1. Select Screens locks kinds from your Settings by tapping on Lock screen >, then choose a protected screen lock (PIN, Pattern, or Password).

2. To enable the display of alerts on your lock screen, tap �. The choices that are accessible are as follows:

- Hide contents: This feature aids in hiding the alerts that appear in your Notification panel.
- Notifications to show: Assists in choosing which notification appears on your lock screen.

3. Select Done and then close your menu.

4. Configure the following screen lock options:

- Smart Lock: When your phone recognizes other devices or secure areas, this function unlocks it immediately. Secured screen lock is required for this function.
- Secured lock settings: Adjust your secured lock's settings. Secured screen lock is required for this function.
- Lock screen: To change the look and contents of your lock screen, you should Touch.
- Widgets: Tap to change the widgets that appear next to the clock on your Lock screen.

- Press and hold to edit: Choose whether to allow things on your lock screen to be edited with a touch or hold.

- Roaming clock: This shows you the time at home and wherever you are when you're out and about.

- What is the lock screen? Your lock screen's software needs to be updated.

Google Play Protect

You may configure Google Play to automatically scan your apps for hazards and security issues on your device.

o Select ⬤ Security & privacy > App security > Google's Play Protects from your Settings.

- An automated update check is performed.

Install unknown apps

You can allow specific sites or apps to install unknown third-party applications.

1. Select ⬤ Security & privacy > Install unfamiliar applications from the Settings menu.

2. Press to allow installation from the program or source.

TIP: Unauthorized third-party program installations may raise the risks to your mobile device's security and the privacy of your data.

Accounts

You can access and control every account you have, including social media, email, and Google and Samsung accounts.

Adding an account

You may add and synchronize all of your social networking, email, and picture and video sharing accounts.

1. Select Accounts & backup > Manage accounts > Add account from the Settings menu.

2. Select an account type from the list.

3. Follow the setup steps to create an account, input your login information, and choose "Auto sync data" to have your accounts update automatically.

Account preferences

Every account has a unique collection of preferences. It is possible to define standard configurations for all accounts of the same kind. The features and account settings offered vary depending on the kind of account.

1. Tap 🔄 Accounts & backup > and then choose Manage accounts from your Settings.

2. To change the settings, tap on any account.

Remove an account

You have the option to delete an account from the gadget.

1. Select 🔄 Accounts & backup > Manage accounts from the Settings menu

2. Select your account and then select "Remove account."

Backup and restore

You may configure your device to keep private account data backups on it.

153

Samsung account

It is possible to enable data backups for your Samsung account. Service providers could present a range of choices.

- o After selecting ⟲ Accounts & Backup from your Settings, you can select one of the following from within your Samsung Cloud:

- Data backup: Create a Samsung account to save data backups.

- Restore the data: Go into your Samsung account on your smartphone to access your backup data.

Google account

You have the option to allow data backups to your Google Account.

1. Go to Settings and choose ⟲ Accounts & backup.

2. Select Back-up data from the Google Drive menu.

External storage transfer

You have two options for recovering backup data: either utilize Smart Switch or backup your data to an SD card or USB device. Select Accounts & backup > Externals storage transfers from the Settings menu.

Google settings

You may customize your Google settings by selecting from the choices provided, which are dependent on the Google Accounts you use.

o Select Ⓖ Google from your Settings, then select any personalization option.

Troubleshooting

When necessary, you can reset the services on your device and search for software updates.

Software update/System update

Software updates are always available for you to look for and then install on your device. Service providers could present a range of choices.

o To access these choices, choose System update/Software updates from your Settings:

- Update checks: This facilitates the manual search for software updates.

- Keep posting updates: The halted update can now be continued.

Reset

Reset the network settings and your devices. You can also return the gadget to its original settings.

Reset all settings

Everything on your device has been reset to its original factory settings, with the exception of your language, security, and account settings. Private data is not impacted.

1. Select ⬚ General management from the Settings menu, then touch Reset and finally Reset-all settings.

2. Tap the Reset settings button, and when prompted, confirm.

Reset network settings

You may reset Wi-Fi, Bluetooth, and mobile data settings using the Resets networks settings.

1. Select General management from the Settings menu, then press Reset and finally Resets networks configuration.

2. Tap Reset settings, and when requested, confirm.

Reset accessibility settings

You can reset the accessibility settings on your device. There won't be any impact on the accessibility settings from your personal data or the programs you downloaded.

1. To reset the accessibility settings, go to Settings, touch ⬌ General Management, then pick Reset.

2. Tap Reset settings, and when requested, confirm

Factory Data Reset

Resetting your smartphone to its original settings will remove all of its data.

This step permanently deletes all of the device's data, including music, photographs, videos, system, Google or extra account settings, downloaded programs, application data & settings, and other files. Any data stored on a second SD card is unaffected.

When you customize your lock screen on your device while logged into your Google account, your Google Devices Protections are activated immediately.

NOTE: Resetting the password on a Google account can take up to 24 hours to become effective on all connected devices.

Before resetting your device:

1. Verify that the information you want to save has moved into the storage space.

2. Check your user name and password by signing into your Google account.

To reset your device:

1. Select General management > Reset > Factory data resets from your Settings menu.

2. To do your reset, tap Reset and then follow the instructions.

3. When your device resumes, complete the setup steps.

Google Device Protection

After you set up lock screen and log into any Google Account on your mobile device, your Google Devices Protection becomes active. This service protects your phone from an unintentional factory data wipe by using your Google account information to verify your identity.

Enable Google Device Protection

As soon as you connect a Google Account and set a lock screen on your smartphone, Google Devices Protection becomes active.

Disable Google Device Protection

To disable Google Devices Protection, you may either erase your lock screen or remove all of your Google Accounts from your device.

Follow these steps to delete your Google accounts:

1. Select Manage accounts > then [Google Account] after tapping on 🔄 Accounts & backup in your Settings.

2. Select "Remove account."

To remove a secure lock screen:

1. Navigate to Settings, hit 🔒 Lock screen, and then choose Screen locks type.

2. Press the Swipe or None button.

www.ingramcontent.com/pod-product-compliance
Lightning Source LLC
LaVergne TN
LVHW051240050326
832903LV00028B/2492